STRP
An
Adventurous
Life

FATHER

STRP
An Adventurous Life

MARK HOPKINS

Book design by the author

ISBN 9798872696018

Library of Congress Control Number 2024902721

This book is dedicated to those bacterial
companions whose myriad beneficial
generations thriving within the author
have escorted him through so many
years of good health and happiness.

STRP
An
Adventurous
Life

Hello. I'm STRP. That's just how we are called. My father was BRFT. Scientists who study my kind wouldn't know that. They would call me *bacillophipyllis polymathii,* whatever that means. But no, I am just STRP, and I am from a proud family with ancient roots. We're a beneficial woodland clan, by the way; none of those awful infectious-disease-perpetrating scoundrels disgrace our ranks.

My normal lifespan is 36 hours at most, and I was born in a lovely splotch of decaying leaf litter high on a branch of a tree on my tiny oceanic island. That's me, snuggled down at bottom center, having my lunch. But you cannot see me, because I am invisible to the naked eye. Human eye, that is.

Those scientists don't know that I can see. But I can. Perfectly. And I have seen many things. For example, this was my first view of the world when I was born yesterday just as the dawn broke. What an absolute delight it was to witness that gorgeous sight.

Later, I watched for hours as fleecy clouds drifted by and left me wondering what they are made of and whether they're edible.

Around noontime a passing lady bug
crawled right smack over me. It made
me wonder if all ladybugs use the same
pronoun. But I didn't know how to ask.

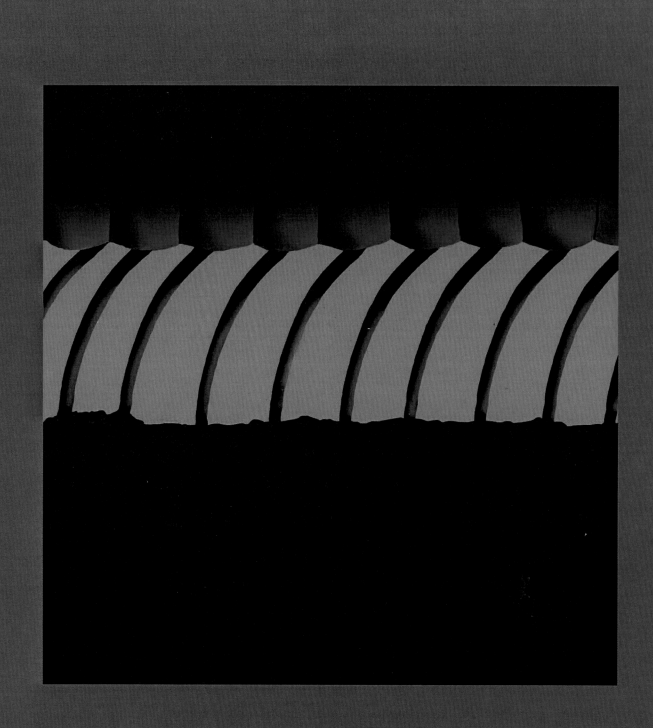

Shortly after, a wandering millipede came slithering down my branch and for a moment gave me quite a caged view. A few of those amazing feet nearly impaled me. I tasted one. Fffft! Who eats that?

It was a quiet and uneventful day as I munched on delectable leaf litter and watched the sun soar in its daily arc across the heavens. As it set at the island's other end far behind me, I marveled at the wonderfully gentle colors that bedecked the eastern sky.

When the sky darkened and nighttime descended upon us, the stars came out and I was overwhelmed. Such singular beauty!

Later in the night an owl swooped in and perched on my branch, totally enveloping me and subsequently informing me that feathers have negligible nutrient value. Happily it had business elsewhere and soon flew away.

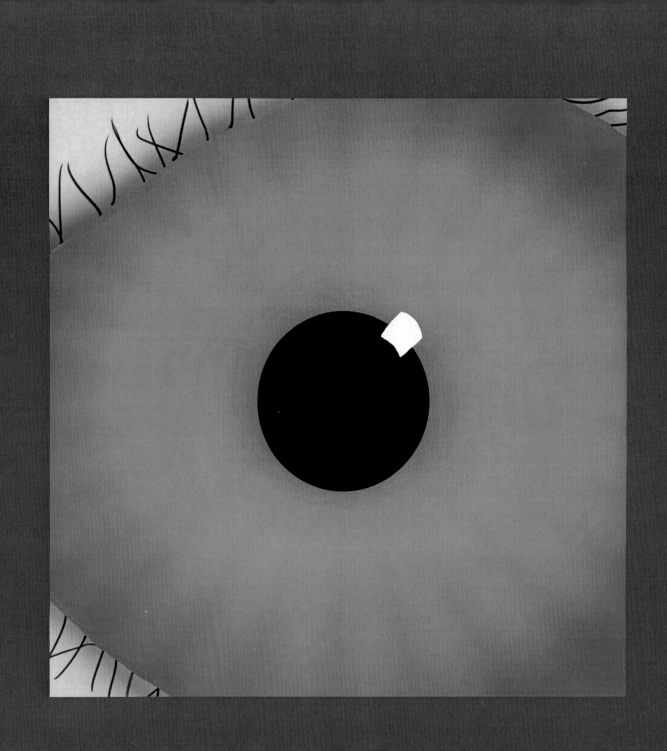

Yesterday another wonderous thing happened, by the way: I saw a naked eye. It belonged to a passing human collecting mushrooms. It never saw me, though, and I was parked right next to some luscious spores of a chanterelle. I carefully nudged them into the humus below me to assure their future growth.

After that memorable sighting yesterday, I rolled face down into the darkness
of the leaf litter below and listened to
the munchings of thousands of fellow
bacteria busily fulfilling their given roles.
Their very presence filled me with patri-
otic pride. It was here that I regretted
my microscopic size; if larger I could
have dragged palm fronds over my
colleagues to protect them from the
heat of the morning sun.

As I lay there, an earthworm thrust its head (or was it its tail?) out from the leaf litter and towered over me. But it had nothing to say. I wondered what its life down under must be like without eyes to see, ears to hear, or a nose to sniff things with. Surely it must have had a mouth, although I certainly couldn't detect anything that looked like one.

My first night passed quickly, and then
came the day of my amazing adventures.
Just at sunrise I was perched on a leaf
fragment admiring the dawning sky
and relishing a delighful breakfast of
rancid fungus when it began.

A delicate, warm breeze drifted upward
from the sea. Magically it lifted us --
me and my leaf chip -- gently aloft.
Suddenly we were flying! Free and clear!

There I was immersed in the gray of dawn, perched comfortably on a tiny flying carpet and gliding away from my woodland birthplace. It was exhilarating! I wondered what other marvels lay ahead.

And so began a voyage more beautiful than I could imagine. I'll be quiet now and let you savor the marvelous sights I saw.

Isn't it gorgeous the way the landscape catches those luscious dawn hues?

.....floating, floating.....

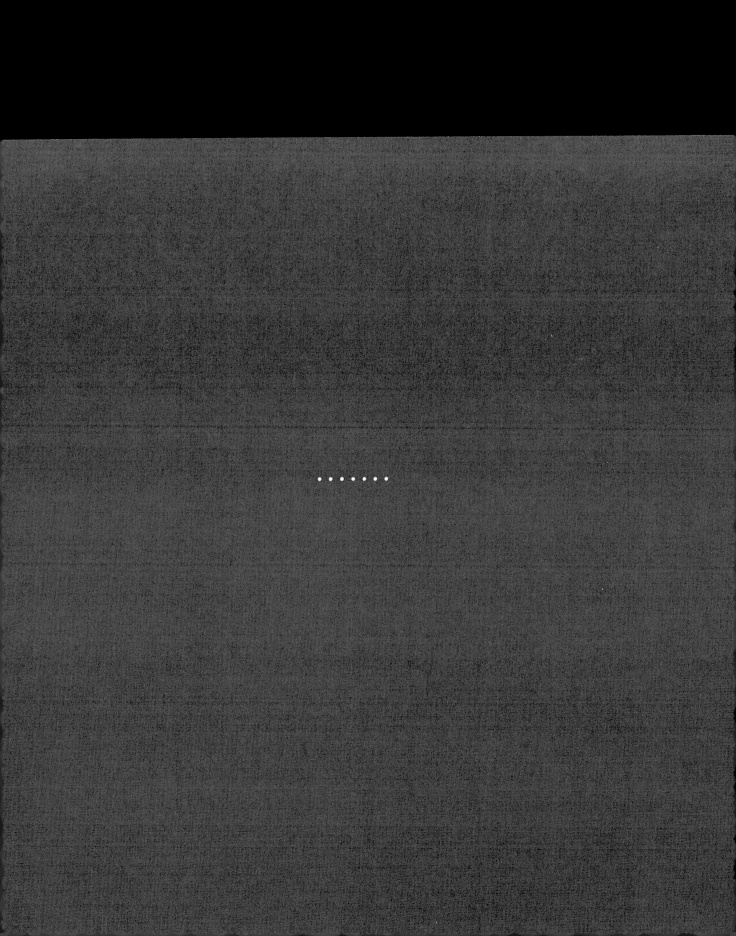

But WHOA!! Just then we drifted up to a steep cliff, and when we soared over the edge of it......

.....a sudden unexpected downdraft
caught us. In the turmoil I was blown
off my tiny carpet and found myself
drifting uncontrollably on a breeze
that was carrying me toward the sea.

Oh dear, this is not good, I thought.
There was endless ocean down there.
Not an ideal destination for one my
size, especially since I didn't know if
I floated or not.

But there is hope, I surmised; perhaps
I could snag onto one of those two trees.
It was terrifying when I considered the
consequences of passing through them
and on to my demise. I veered closer
and closer.....

....when suddenly a tiny breeze back-swirled and I found myself headed for a flowery landing, I wondered what those big yellow ones would taste like.

Crash site ahead!! Hang on!

And there I was, all in one piece and nosed into a scramble of bizarre looking flower parts. I took a nibble or two but everything was far too organically fresh for my taste.

I had no more than settled down when an exploring ant crawled over me, stepping on me as it passed. It left quite a dent in my side, but I popped it out successfully. What could be next?

It didn't take long to find out. A gigan-
tic honey bee zoomed in and plopped
onto the flower, busy collecting pollen
for its hive.

The bee scooped up every pollen grain in sight, which (aaargh) included me caught in the sticky middle of it all. Then, with a great gush of buzzing, it took off and was airborne again. I nib-bled a pollen grain as we gained altitude. Urrf, much too sweet.

But the bee didn't get far. WHAM!! A hungry bird unexpectedly swooped out of the sky and nabbed it for an airborne snack. In the turmoil that followed, all those pollen grains were scattered far and wide. And me with them.

So once again here I was, out of control
and gliding grandly through the air
toward the open ocean and who knew
what fate. Grimly, this time there was
nothing to snag onto along the way.
This was going to be a wet one.

With the tiniest plop you can imagine,
I landed on the open ocean. Happily, the
sea was calm so there were no waves to
battle. And , luckily for me, I discover-
ed that we float. But this was a chilling
exercise. Brrrr. And who knew what
untold horrors lurked in those murky
depths below.

Fortuitously, a mild onshore breeze was pushing me along, and it wasn't long before the beach loomed large and I was being swept onto it.

Sandy tropical beaches are not exactly luxurious when you're my size. This is how beach sand looked to me. And it's treacherous, because there is always the risk of tumbling down into one of those crevices never to be seen again.

The tide quickly receded and the tropical sun was relentless. Oh my, wasn't it hot on that beach! It was *searing*! I was baking. What else could possibly go wrong?

Right where I had landed there rested a tiny dead minnow that the tide had washed up. I squiggled into its shadow for relief, and gave the minnow a lick. Ugh! Far too fishy. I was beginning to realize I'm a vegetarian through and through. But wait!! Look what was approaching from down the beach.

Drat!! Stepped on again! The seagull gathered up the little minnow, gobbled it down, and then took off into the sky with me stuck to a wet spot on the bottom of its foot. Now what??

We gained altitude quickly, and I had to admit that the view was magnificent. But the rushing air quickly dried my sticky wet spot and, having no limbs with which to hang on, I -- horrors!! -- tumbled off. Here I was, flying again. And all that was below me now was a vast expanse of wild forest. This did not look good.

A stately hawk soared just beneath me and, as I dropped, I missed by inches landing on one of its wings. I wondered where that would have taken me. But there I was, still falling fast.

Wild forest lay below in every direction. And nothing I could see ressembled a favorable landing site. This ongoing airborne business was getting tedious for a ground dweller, especially a tiny one. I continued to plummet.

The forest canopy was coming up fast, and I wondered if I could slip through all those treetops and safely work my way down to leaf litter level. Get ready, I told myself; this is likely to take some wild maneuvering.

Holding my breath, I took a deep dive into the canopy. The last thing I needed was to spend the rest of my life hung up in those forbidding tree tops, so it took some fancy twisting and turning as I passed through the crown and plunged deep into the shadows of primeval forest.

Happily I floated easily through the interlocking foliage. And what a menagerie was there to greet me. The chitterings and warbles of sweet birdsong resounded everywhere. As I floated past this tree snake hunting for its next meal, I recalled that snakes swallow furry mammals whole and wondered if flavor was even an issue for them.

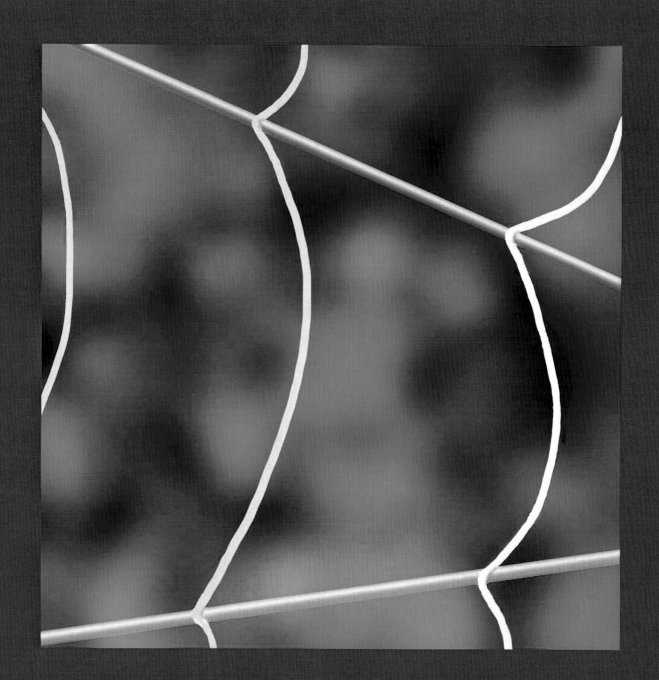

Spider web ahead!! Luckily I drifted
right through without touching a strand.
While spiders could care less about a
quarry my size, those filaments are sur-
prisingly sticky and you don't want to
spend the rest of your life inadver-
tently stuck to one.

On the way I floated past this highway
of ants headed for the canopy. I won-
ered what they had going for themselves
up there and what it tasted like.

I knew I was invisible to this ruby-eyed menace but I was nevertheless terrified to see that enormous mouth that I knew was capable of gobbling down any living thing that it could cram into it. And so my journey continued downward.

I drifted past a covey of bats draped
from a branch, wrapped in their wings
and contentedly snoozing the day away.
One eye popped open but I doubted
that it noticed the passing dust mote
that was me. I considered their dietary
preferences and wondered how anyone
could endure an entire lifetime of eating
bugs.   Blecch.

Another tree loomed below and there on a branch, to my profound delight, crawled the perfect landing site: a beautifully squishy caterpillar. With a few clumsy squiggles I tweaked my glide-path and succeeded in executing a perfect one-point landing on its cushiony and very colorful back. It never so much as noticed my arrival.

It was so soft and comfortable there,
and my adventures had so overwhelmed
me, that I snuggled down for a brief
and very welcomed snooze.

But it was not to be. I had no more
than drifted off when there arose a
great commotion and I barely missed
seeing an absolutely spectacular bird
exploding upward through the foliage.
What exquisite tail feathers it had!! I
wondered what the rest of it must
have looked like.

Then, without missing a beat, look what
came galumphing along the branch and
burst out from under the palm fronds.
A forest chameleon! From the looks of it,
a very hungry one. And as everyone in
these parts knew, fat caterpillars were
its favorite delicacies. This did not look
good at all.

That great cavernous mouth slowly gaped
open and out loomed its dreaded weapon:
the fearsome pink, sticky, spring-loaded
tongue that it used to capture and swallow
its prey. There was a moment's pause as
it fine-tuned its aim, and then......

SPLAT!!! We were instantly immobilized.
Captured! Goners!! Without hesitation
that revolting tongue snapped back into
the gaping mouth, dragging me and the
caterpillar along with it. Now what?

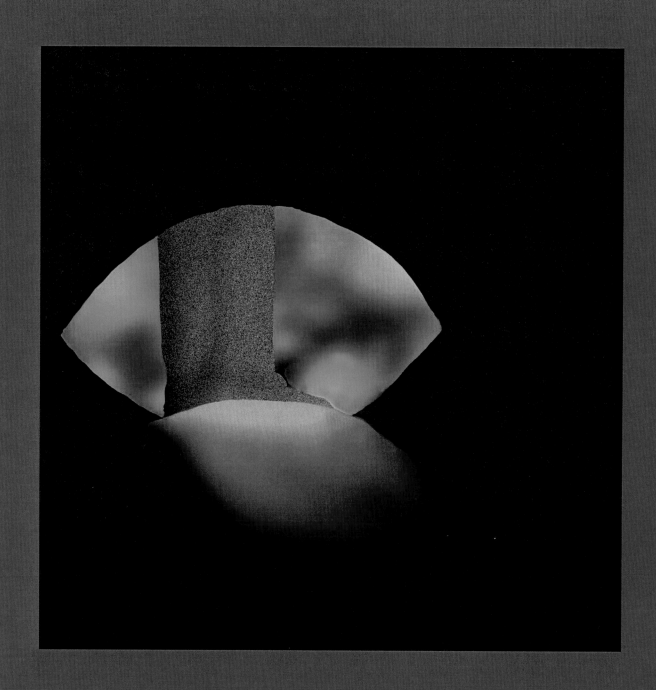

Looking over my shoulder, (I'm allowed
to say that even though I don't have one),
I watched that terrifying tongue reassem--
ble itself back into the mouth as those
enormous jaws closed with a snap and
suddenly......

.....here I was, despite it still being early morning, immersed once again in the darkest of night. This was truly a dilemma, but I clearly had no choice but to settle back and wait for whatever was next to befall me.

Time seemed to go on forever. We waited. And we waited. I should say, I waited, because the caterpillar at this point
appeared to be mysteriously dissolving
away beneath me. I nuzzled it reassur-
ingly but doubted that I provided any
solace.

Things were definitely not pleasant in there. It was wet and squishy. It smelled funny. And what were all those weird gurgling sounds? What to do?? I wondered if this was how it was all supposed to end.....and when.

But wait!! A spot of daylight suddenly loomed in the distance!! A light at the end of the, er, tunnel ?? What could this mean? What was going to happen now?

Things moved very rapidly then, and in a flash (actually it was more like a flush) there I was, immersed in the warmth of the late afternoon sunlight, happily deposited onto another leaf litter patch, quite sticky and badly in need of a bath.

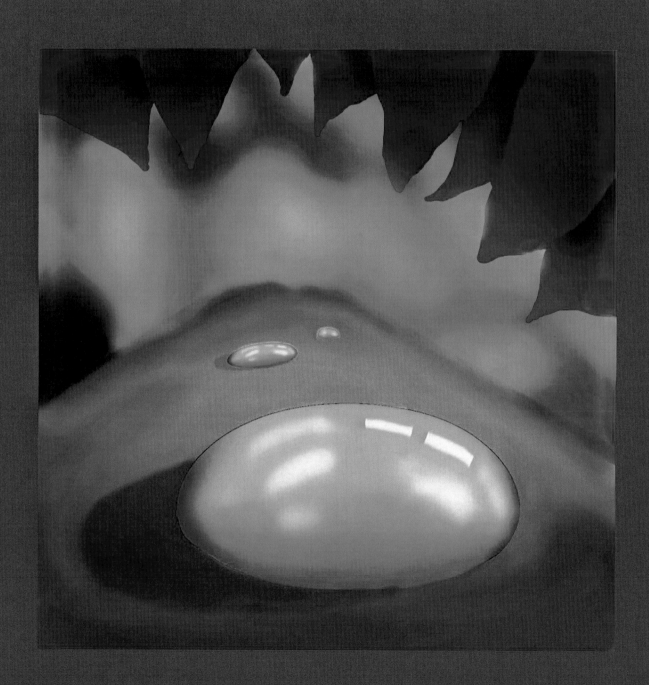

Apparently there had been a sprinkle while we were inside, because scattered here and there were little shimmering raindrops. I eagerly dove into the closest one, rinsed mself off, had a nice swim, and emerged to dry myself off and indulge in a long-awaited meal.

I didn't have far to look. Towering over me was an elegant mushroom clearly poised at the edge of turning rancidly putrid, which is exactly the way I like them. As I rolled over to savor the delicious opportunity, a tiny maggot, progeny of those houseflies, pushed past me and dug in. I carefully repositioned myself so that we could both share the feast together.

Oh, the joy and comfort of a full belly!!
I belched contentedly, loud enough to
startle a formidable looking spider that
had been snoozing nearby and popped
up to assess the disturbance. I wondered how spiders can sleep while having
so many eyes they cannot shut.

While I was hunkered down a wandering
rodent -- I think a vole -- scampered
right over me, all the while munching a
mouthful of greens. Happily it didn't
step on me once. Judging from the
white of those whiskers and given its
impeccable manners, it must have been
a venerable old-timer.

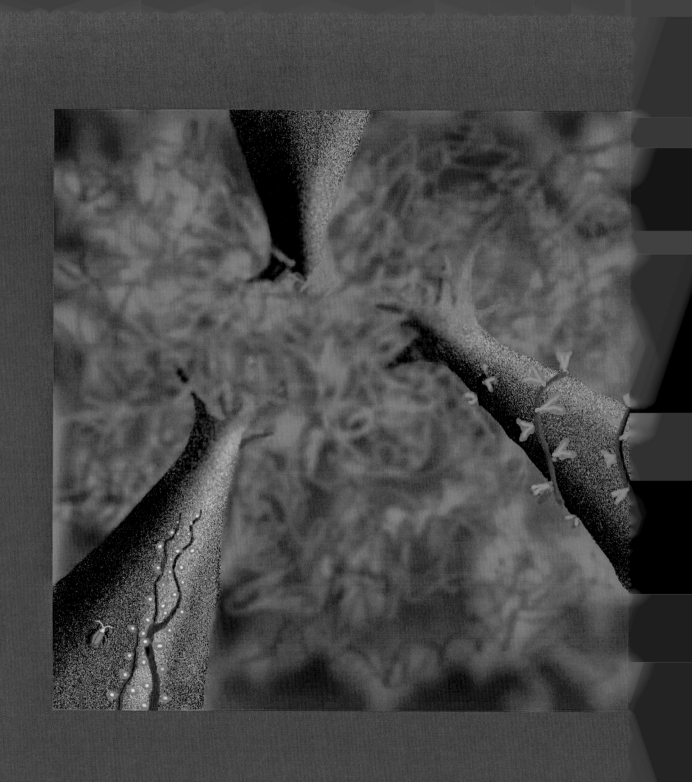

Sated, I lay gazing contentedly at the lovely canopy above and rejoicing to hear the warm murmurs of a thousnd microbes bedded all around me. Scientists who study us haven't yet realized how well we communicate intuitively. It'll come. And they'll pro-bably call it *intuitalisation* or some such pompous sesquipedalian term. We don't need a word for it because we don't need words to communicate. That's how advanced we are.

But wait! The colors were changing.
Everything was taking on a reddish hue.
The light was fading. The day was ending.
I quickly rolled over to look behind me.....

......and there I beheld the most spectacular sight I could possibly imagine.
What splendor!   What a beautiful
world this was!   And how lucky I was to
have had my time here.   I watched
in wonder as the constantly evolving,
dazzling colors fanned out in their glory
across the western sky.

And so my time had come. That certainly was an event-filled life for a modest
bacillophipyllis polymathii. Think about
it. I ventured out and about. Took some
risks. Saw some surprising aspects of
the world. Had some adventures. Even
toured an alimentary canal. And along
with all that, I enjoyed the satisfaction
of doing some good things for others.

So much to reflect on. Such fulfillment!
Such joy! I could have written a book!
A book? By a mere microorganism?
Sheesh. But now I must turn to inner
matters because, as we say in bacterial
circles, life goes on but we don't. The
time has come. Time to split.

STRP signing out. Live well.